THE
Ann E. Answers
Guide to
Communications
Etiquette
in the Digital Age

THE

Ann E. Answers

Guide to

Communications
Etiquette

in the Digital Age

By the Staff of Goff Public

Mill City Press, Inc.
322 First Avenue N, 5th floor
Minneapolis, MN 55401
612.455.2293
www.millcitypublishing.com

ISBN-13: 978-1-62652-298-5
LCCN: 2013914942

Cover Design by Alan Pranke
Typeset by James Arneson

Printed in the United States of America.

Contents

Chapter 3 Update Status
Engaging in a hyper-connected world............ *33*

Chapter 4 Refresh
Vintage communications to impress a modern audience *55*

Chapter 5 Write Once, Revise Twice
Creating meaningful content............................ *65*

Chapter 6 Approve This Message
Mastering the art of political participation .. 87

Chapter 7 Click to Apply
Making the right impression 103

Preface

In the past two decades, innovations in technology have created previously unimaginable changes in the ways we communicate and store information. The pace of business has quickened. Vast oceans of knowledge, opinion and entertainment beckon to be swum in (and threaten to drown us). Journalistic and political gatekeepers are more skeptically regarded and perhaps more accountable, though they, too, have more tools to keep tabs on us.

It is no exaggeration to say that life for billions of people has been transformed in myriad ways – and is still being transformed. It is almost as though the revolutionary changes wrought over centuries by the printing press, telegraph, radio, and television all have occurred within the span of just a few years.

Our new means of talking, writing and exchanging information have reshaped many of the ways we interact with each other in daily life. But we, the communicators, still rely on social conventions which are firmly rooted, for the most part, in ancient forms of human communication, including face-to-face encounters, handshakes to punctuate agreement, and handwritten thank-you notes.

Today, two very different populations are working side by side in business, education, civic and cultural settings. One entered the workforce before the Internet and its progeny existed, the other after their advent. Each generation has slightly different takes on appropriate business behavior and norms of conduct. Each can learn from the other how to adapt our modern convenient tools to the conventions of common courtesy, good taste, and considerateness in everyday communications.

We at Goff Public strive to be at the forefront of communications advances, from multimedia platforms to social media to video production, while still practicing the timeless arts of message development, persuasive writing, traditional media relations, and coalition building. As we embrace and use new technologies, we have found ourselves asking and answering questions about how to properly employ new tools alongside the traditional ones.

We developed "Ann E. Answers" as the fun personification of our own struggle for the right responses to questions about etiquette in this digital age. She is young enough to be fluent in the latest digital trends, but mature and experienced in her judgments. As you read this book, you will find that Ann E. Answers has strong, sometimes tart opinions on our daily behaviors in the business world and beyond, from the right time to "friend" someone on Facebook to the proper use of emoticons to the correct use of an out-of-office reply. You may disagree with some of her advice, but when you do, we hope she will stimulate your thinking about the right practices.

The Ann E. Answers Guide to Communications Etiquette in the Digital Age can help you carry yourself appropriately in the 21st century. Whether you spend a big part of your day navigating social media sites or you feel like a communications Luddite, we hope your thoughts are provoked and you have some fun in the process.

Chris Georgacas
President and Chief Executive Officer
Goff Public, Inc.

Introduction

Viral energy. E-mail blasts. Crowdsourcing. Social content curation. Organic conversations. These buzzwords are just some of the industry jargon that represent how important e-communications have become over the past decade. But the onslaught of new technologies – from social media to smartphones – can be both a blessing and a curse for the business world.

People who grew up in the age of rotary phones and black-and-white TV might find it hard to communicate with the tech-savvy, social media-oriented 20-somethings who are joining the modern workplace (and vice versa). While older generations might think that constantly updating your Twitter account on your smartphone is rude, younger people might see this as a normal part of everyday life.

We need a set of rules that govern business communication in the Internet age. That's where I come riding in on a shiny iPad to save the day.

While I appreciate the strategic benefits which social media and e-communications provide businesses – especially the ability to communicate more effectively with the people who matter most – I also understand that seemingly old-school communications methods, like a handwritten thank-you note, are often the best way to impact someone.

This book is a compilation of advice that I have provided to people on how to appropriately use digital communications in a professional setting. From managing day-to-day communications with colleagues and clients to making quality connections on social media to communicating with public officials, I'll make sure that you don't inadvertently harm a relationship, or your reputation, by committing an e-communications *faux pas*.

The general rules and principles which I have laid out in this book should help you address many questions that arise related to modern-day communications etiquette. But if you are still stumped, please e-mail me at: anneanswers@goffpublic.com.

Check Messages

Perfecting the daily fundamentals

E-mail salutations and closings

Dear Ann E. Answers:

A longtime acquaintance recently became one of my clients. I'm now really in a quandary! How formal should my business e-mails be to someone I already know? Do I need to start with "Dear So-and-So" and close with "Sincerely" or "Best Wishes"?

Sincerely,

Formality in Doubt

Dear Formality in Doubt:
Don't get too wrapped up in pomp and circumstance.

Most e-mails can be fairly informal, especially when you e-mail someone you know. Even so, you should still lead with the person's name – either "Sally," or "Hello/Hi, Sally," – before getting to the point. There might be times, like during a quick exchange of several e-mails, when leading with the person's name isn't essential, but it is still a nice touch to regularly practice.

The closing doesn't have to be as formal as "Sincerely," and can even be as simple as "Thank you," or "I look forward to hearing from you."

However, if you or your client has a more formal disposition, a salutation and closing may be perfectly natural in your e-mails.

Of course, a more formal approach is most appropriate if you are e-mailing a person or group whom you have not met, or if you're contacting them unexpectedly or for the first time via e-mail.

Should I use an out-of-office reply?

Dear Ann E. Answers:

I'm leaving for a two-week vacation soon, which is longer than any vacation I've taken at my current job. I've never left an out-of-office reply on my e-mail before, but now I think I might need one, especially since I have new responsibilities at work. What do you think?

Sincerely,

Unsure Vacationer

Dear Unsure Vacationer:

As with a lot of business etiquette questions, whether or not you should use an out-of-office e-mail reply depends on your line of work, your position within the company, and how quickly people typically need to reach you.

A good rule is that if you are going to deviate from your normal response rate, you should notify people that they will probably not hear back from you in a timely fashion.

There are certain times when you might be out of the office, but do not need to set an out-of-office reply. If you are going on a business trip and will be able to respond to e-mails regularly, you don't need an out-of-office reply. Additionally, it is not necessary to set an out-of-office reply during weekends and holidays.

If you decide to use an out-of-office reply, you should provide the name of an alternative contact person or your office's general phone number and indicate whether you will access your e-mail while you're gone.

Some people also like to state the date(s) that they will be out of the office or when they will return. (This practice, however, is dictated partly by personal security considerations.) You do not need to give an explanation as to why you are out of the office.

You may also want to change your voicemail. Only provide your cell phone number if you are willing to take business calls when you are out of the office. Otherwise, provide the name and number of an alternative contact in your office who can take the call(s).

Most importantly, remember to disable your out-of-office reply and change your voicemail message when you get back.

When to use blind copies

Dear Ann E. Answers:

I have recently been "blind carbon copied" on a number of work e-mails and am a bit confused about its purpose. I have never blind copied anyone on an e-mail and am wondering in what types of situations it is appropriate.

Sincerely,

Nothing to Hide

Dear Nothing to Hide:

I understand your confusion. On the surface, using a blind carbon copy (bcc) sounds like a form of electronic deception – and it can be, if used inappropriately. A bcc should only be used in a very limited capacity, and there should never be any intent to deceive. But there are certainly some circumstances when it is okay to use this feature.

- If you are sending an e-mail to a client and one of your coworkers who has not met the client needs to be kept in the loop, a bcc is a great way to make that colleague aware of the e-mail without confusing your client.
- If you are sending a work-related e-mail where the list of recipients must remain confidential, a bcc is an efficient option because you can reach all of the recipients in one e-mail.
- A bcc can also be used if it is unnecessary for recipients of a mass e-mail to know who else is receiving the e-mail.
- A bcc can be used to prevent someone from "replying all," which may not be appropriate for all recipients

and could cause conflict. But beware! Make sure you won't be embarrassed in front of your main recipients if an inattentive bcc recipient "replies all."

Using a bcc in forwarded e-mails can prevent spam. For example, if you receive a mass e-mail from a friend with 25 recipients, spammers who get their hands on the e-mail will now have 25 more e-mail addresses to add to their lists. Additionally, the potential for spam increases as the e-mail is forwarded to more people.

If the sender instead uses the bcc feature, recipient e-mail addresses are less likely to appear in other people's inboxes and be susceptible to spam. Good e-mail forwarders also take the time to remove all existing e-mail addresses within the body of the message.

Should I e-mail or call?

Dear Ann E. Answers:

When I want to talk to someone, I'd rather pick up the phone than send an e-mail. However, I feel like my colleagues often get quicker responses from people when they use e-mail. Is it just me, or has e-mail replaced the phone as most people's preferred method of business communication?

Sincerely,

Phone-Using Dinosaur

Dear Phone-Using Dinosaur:

I respect your old-school tactics, and I believe the phone call still has value. The phone vs. e-mail debate in some ways defines a generational clash between pre-Internet and post-Internet professionals. People born after 1990 don't remember a world when e-mail didn't exist. As more of the Internet generation enters the workforce, the preference for e-mail may only increase. But that's not to say the "old-school" phone call doesn't have its advantages for professionals of any generation.

Many sales professionals say they have a higher success rate when they contact prospective customers over the phone as opposed to e-mail. One of the reasons may be that it's more difficult to hang up on someone than it is to delete an e-mail. But the bigger reason is the human element. While e-mails are just words on a screen, a person calling has a voice with a real personality. It can be difficult to understand how people feel through e-mail correspondence. But with phone conversations, you can make inferences about the speaker's mood or mind-set on a particular matter from his or her tone of voice and inflection.

Another situation where phone trumps e-mail is when time is a factor. If someone calls you, this person either prefers phone calls to e-mails in general or believes the reason for the call warrants a give-and-take conversation – which has the potential to get very tedious over e-mail. Further, highly sensitive information often shouldn't be communicated in writing.

E-mail has plenty of upsides as well. Many people are more comfortable with e-mail because they are able to control when they read and respond to messages. While phone calls require quick responses from both parties (and can sometimes result in a frustrating game of "phone tag"), e-mailing gives people time to mull over the most appropriate way to respond before replying. E-mails are easy to organize so you can look back at prior conversations to remember what was said. This can't be done with phone calls unless you have a court reporter documenting your every word! Finally, business agreements should never be made official just over the phone. While the initial terms can be agreed upon in a phone call, the finalized agreement needs a paper (or in certain cases, an electronic) trail.

Sometimes a simple face-to-face discussion is more appropriate than either an e-mail or phone call, especially within an office. Employees usually hate to be "managed by e-mail," and supervisors generally learn more about subordinates through regular human interaction. (See

"Deciphering nonverbal communication" on page 16 for more information.)

Most people have a preferred means of communication, and it's acceptable to ask people for theirs. Once you have determined that preference, respect it.

The average business e-mail account received 89 messages per day in 2012, a number which is expected to grow to 144 messages daily by 2016.

The Radicati Group, "E-mail Statistics Report, 2012-2016," (April 2012).

How to leave a good voicemail

Dear Ann E. Answers:

I recently landed a job where I am required to make a lot of phone calls to clients and vendors. I want to make a good impression right away to ensure my call is returned. Do you have any tips for leaving a good voicemail?

Sincerely,

Voicemail Rookie

Dear Voicemail Rookie:
Leaving voicemails doesn't have to be complicated. The first thing you should know is that people can detect uncertainty in a person's voice. When your call goes to voicemail, be confident in what you say. Uncertainty leads to hesitation, awkward pauses, unnecessary fillers like "um" and "uh," and the greater likelihood that your call will not be returned.

In order to avoid this, plan ahead when placing a call. Before you pick up the phone to dial, you should already have an idea of what you are planning to say whether you connect with the person whom you are calling or need to leave a voicemail. I find it helpful to write out the key points that I want to convey in case I am directed to a voicemail box. That way I can make sure I convey all the details and know just what to say next. But you also don't want to be scripted to the point where you sound like a generic voice recording.

Part of having phone confidence means being able to use your own wording on the spot to fluently convey your message. This comes with practice.

Here is what you should include in your voice message: your name, the purpose of your call, a call to action for the receiver, and – arguably most important – your phone number and/or e-mail address, depending on your preferred method of contact. Make sure you speak clearly and slowly. It never hurts to provide your name and contact information twice so the listener doesn't have to listen to the voicemail a second time.

Remember, the world is flooded with communications – e-mail, voicemail, and regular mail – so don't take it personally if you have to call a few times to get a response.

If you need a timely response, consider sending an e-mail in addition to leaving a voicemail message. Covering all of the bases will help you learn the best way to reach that person.

> Most professionals recommend keeping a voicemail to 30 seconds or less, if possible. Short, clear messages are more likely to engage a listener's attention and result in a callback.

Why you need a smartphone e-mail signature

Dear Ann E. Answers:

I have a bone to pick with my smartphone-using friends and colleagues. I'm tired of seeing "Sent from my iPhone" or "Sent from my Android" at the bottom of people's e-mails. I get it: you're awesome; you have a smartphone. Do you really need to broadcast it to the whole world?

Sincerely,

iPhone Envy

Dear iPhone Envy:

Maybe you're jealous of the millions of other Americans with smartphones. But it's time for you to realize that iPhone users are not necessarily bragging about their smartphones. Rather, they are sharing this information as a way to easily excuse abbreviated e-mails sent from smartphones, which can be cumbersome to type on.

Let's say, for example, a client sent you a short e-mail from an iPhone that read "Need you to make that edit ASAP." If you didn't realize that person was sending an e-mail from his or her smartphone, you might misconstrue the tone of the e-mail or question the person's professionalism.

If you do get a smartphone and you are still worried that you will sound like you are bragging about your newfound tool, try using the e-mail signature "Sent from my iPhone. Please excuse my brevity."

While the smartphone signature covers for concision and minor grammatical errors, it should not replace proper spelling and punctuation.

Almost half of American adults own smartphones.

Pew Internet & American Life Project, "45% of American adults are smartphone owners," (December 2012).

Check In

Meeting outside the virtual realm

Deciphering nonverbal communication

Dear Ann E. Answers:

I know that body language and facial expressions can be just as important as verbal communication. Can you give me any tips to make sure I'm communicating the right things through my nonverbal actions?

Sincerely,

Nonverbal Communicator

Dear Nonverbal Communicator:
You're right. Nonverbal communication is an extremely important part of human interactions. Without saying a word, you send a distinct message to others through your eyes, gestures and posture. Here are a few tips to improve your nonverbal communications:

Eye contact is critical to good communication because it can reduce tension and convey respect. But don't hold a person's gaze for more than three seconds when first meeting him or her, because too much eye contact can portray aggression, hostility, or even anger. A great tip for direct eye contact is to look into one eye – it looks like direct eye contact, but it's less intense. (Learn more about the importance of eye contact on page 18.)

Make sure you have good posture. Standing or sitting up straight exudes confidence and openness, while slouching indicates a lack of confidence, enthusiasm or interest. Lean toward someone to show that you are interested in what that person has to say.

Be aware of how you hold your hands and arms. Folding your arms during a conversation can signal disinterest or disagreement. It may also appear that you are hiding something. Standing with one hand holding onto the other arm will make you seem unsure. Instead, place your arms comfortably by your side or fold your hands together to display confidence.

Don't cross your legs. Although crossing your legs might be comfortable for you, be aware that doing so signals a negative or defensive attitude. Ideally, you should sit with your legs uncrossed and your feet placed flat on the floor. This sends a message of cooperation, confidence, stability, and friendly interest.

Give a firm, confident handshake. Practice makes perfect – the handshake should be neither a tight squeeze nor a dainty touch. As you reach out, keep in mind that a palm-down position communicates a dominant attitude and palm-up position communicates a submissive demeanor. Therefore, split the difference and keep your hand in a neutral position. The handshake should be no more than three pumps long.

During a conversation, only 7% of the message is conveyed via spoken words. Nonverbal cues, such as appearance, posture, gestures and expression, communicate the majority of information.

Jan Hargrave, *Strictly Business Body Language: Using Nonverbal Communication for Power and Success (Dubuque, Iowa: Hargrave and Associates, 2008)*.

The importance of eye contact

Dear Ann E. Answers:

I pride myself on staying attentive at meetings. One of my coworkers, on the other hand, hardly makes eye contact and gives the impression that he isn't listening. However, when I follow up with him after meetings, it's clear he paid attention. While he apparently is soaking up the information, his nonverbal communication embarrasses me. Should I say something to him? Or am I making too much of his inattentiveness?

Sincerely,

Eyes Don't Lie

Dear Eyes Don't Lie:

If your coworker isn't making regular eye contact during meetings, everyone else in the room is probably thinking the same thing that you are, and, in the process, he's doing a real disservice to his career. No matter the reality of where his head is at, he's screaming, "Get me out of here!"

A person with good eye contact sends a nonverbal message that he is sincere, qualified, personable and focused. Someone who is distracted by his smartphone, gazing aimlessly into space, or half-asleep, however, is sending a message that this meeting is a waste of his time or an opportunity to catch up on other things.

If you consider your coworker a friend, you should tell him that others have noticed his frequent distraction.

Here are some tips for him to follow to clean up his act:

- If you have a smartphone with you, turn off the phone (or at least the volume). The less noise your phone makes, the less distracted you will be. Believe me, even when you think you're being discreet, you aren't.
- Only look down if you are taking notes or looking up relevant information for the meeting.
- Making eye contact is good, but staring is bad. Move your gaze around the table randomly – not clockwise or counterclockwise. Switch your gaze every 5-10 seconds from one person to another (or one eye to the other if you are only with one person).
- The same rules apply to video conferences as in-person meetings.

To learn more about the importance of eye contact and other nonverbal communication cues, see page 16.

Is it okay to respond to an e-mail or text during a meeting?

Dear Ann E. Answers:

Yesterday I was in the middle of a business meeting when I received a text that needed to be addressed immediately. What is the best way to handle such a situation?

Sincerely,

Important Businessperson

Dear Important Businessperson:

My general advice to you: Quit checking your smartphone during meetings. It exudes a sense of arrogance and indifference.

But to answer your question, it depends on how comfortable you are with the people in your meeting. If it's a casual meeting with colleagues, you might be able to get away with responding to an e-mail or text in their presence. In most situations, however, the safest bet is to excuse yourself from the room and return when you are ready to give your undivided attention to the people in the meeting. If you anticipate that a possible interruption might demand your immediate attention, let others in the meeting know in advance.

My general rule, though, is to avoid fiddling with your phone while someone is talking to you. Texting, e-mail checking, and surfing the web while in a group setting – whether it's at a happy hour with friends or at an important meeting – is one of the most common and rudest social behaviors today. Smartphone addicts seem to break this simple rule on an hourly basis. You will stand out by not doing so.

Tips for conducting a successful conference call

Dear Ann E. Answers:

Many of my clients are from other states and countries, so I conduct a lot of meetings via conference call. Between awkward pauses, misinterpretations, and bad technology, I have had my fair share of uncomfortable conference call experiences. Can you shed some light on conference call etiquette to ensure better experiences in the future?

Sincerely,

Over the Speakerphone

Dear Over the Speakerphone:
On the surface, conference calls sound simple. After all, they're just phone calls with more than two people. But since phone calls were originally intended to be an interaction between two people, adding a third, fourth, or tenth person can complicate the call. Below is a list of tips which can put an end to your painful conference call encounters.

- **Send out an agenda beforehand**. Conference calls are more efficient when all participants are on the same page.
- **Don't be late**. Respect everyone's time. It is okay to begin a conference call at the agreed-upon time – even if some of the participants are not on the line.
- **Landlines are better**. Cell phones can result in extraneous noise and dropped calls. Avoid them if possible.

- **Have a conference call moderator**. Select a moderator and let everyone know who he/she is. The moderator's role is to facilitate the flow of the conversation, fill awkward silences, sum up agreements or unresolved items, and – most importantly – manage the collective use of available time.

- **Identify yourself before speaking**. If there are fewer than five people on the call, this rule is only applicable the first time you speak. But if there are five or more people on the call, you should identify yourself every time you speak to avoid confusion among your listeners.

- **Use the mute button if needed**. If you are in a loud place or have a lousy connection, put your phone on mute when you are not speaking to help alleviate noise distractions. No one wants to hear wind noise, background laughter, or – God forbid – someone ordering food at a drive-through during the call!

- **Don't eat**. Your snack can wait until the conference call is over. No one wants to hear you munching on an apple.

- **Treat the call like any other meeting**. Just because call participants can't see you doesn't mean you should surf the Internet or send text messages. Give the conference call your undivided attention.

- **Preset an end time**. Agree on when the call will end and stick to it. If you need to exit the call early, let the moderator know ahead of time.

Keys to a good presentation

Dear Ann E. Answers:

I was asked to give a presentation to my company's shareholders next month. A PowerPoint presentation seems like the easiest route. Do you agree, or is there a better option?

Sincerely,

Uncertain Presenter

Dear Uncertain Presenter:

You were asked to give a presentation – not use PowerPoint. If you think of this task as "giving a PowerPoint presentation," you might as well write random facts on scraps of paper and throw them out to your audience, because each person will probably only absorb a single piece of information.

Don't get me wrong; a PowerPoint presentation can be an effective and interesting tool. But if it is the basis of your entire presentation, you – like many past PowerPoint presenters – might find yourself using it as a crutch rather than as a tool to help enlighten the audience.

I recently wrote a 15-minute presentation that used PowerPoint. The PowerPoint presentation consisted of only eight slides (photos, a basic graph, and a memorable quote). That's because my message was strong enough to stand on its own. I used a PowerPoint presentation for only one reason: to help make my strongest points better resonate with the audience.

My advice is to start by asking yourself why you are being asked to speak and what your audience should learn from it. Then write your outline and practice your comments out loud. Remember to use transitions when you speak, and keep the tone professional, but conversational. After your first rehearsal, determine if a PowerPoint presentation will help make any of your points more effective. A few slides (if any) will likely be all you need.

PowerPoint presentations are seemingly used everywhere and by everyone. But they are often inadequate in helping speakers make understandable or persuasive arguments or informational presentations.

Edward Tufte famously blasted the "cognitive style" of PowerPoint presentations, and others have craved better tools. Alternatives now exist, including free applications and web-based solutions (Prezi is my current favorite).

The use of Microsoft's ubiquitous product is not likely to end anytime soon and can be effective in many situations. But innovative, well-designed alternative platforms are lighting up people's eyes – and minds – in ways which PowerPoint presentations often cannot.

How to request an informational interview

Dear Ann E. Answers:

I recently finished graduate school, and I'm actively looking to re-enter the workforce. I want to approach people for informational interviews. What is the best way to ask someone to meet with me?

Sincerely,

Wannabe Networker

Dear Wannabe Networker:
You are definitely on the right track – connecting with professionals in your industry is one of the most effective things you can do if you are looking for a job or seeking a career change.

Most people are willing to help out young professionals interested in pursuing a career in their field. However, due to their busy schedules, they might not be able to meet with everyone who requests an informational interview. To increase the likelihood that they will network with you, research them on LinkedIn or their company's website. Look for similarities between you and the person: Did the person go to your college? Do you have a mutual friend or acquaintance? If so, you may want to approach the person through your shared connection.

You should always request an informational interview in writing via e-mail or LinkedIn to allow the person to respond at his or her convenience. The message should clearly state that you are not necessarily looking for a job with the person's company, but you are looking for advice on how to get into his or her industry. Set a definite timeframe for how long the meeting should be, and don't request more than 30 minutes for your meeting. Always be willing to meet at or near your contact's workplace. Allow seven to 10 days to get a response to your request before following up.

Before the meeting, you could send your resume in case he or she wants background information about you. Realize that the person probably will not have time to review it. If you are connecting via LinkedIn, it's not necessary to provide a resume because your profile should be your resume. (If it's not, see page 36.)

Getting the most out of an informational interview

Dear Ann E. Answers:

I've finally discovered that I dislike the field I'm in. I'm also scared about getting laid off. So I summoned up the courage to explore another industry. My first informational interview is next week, but I'm starting to get nervous. What should I do during the interview?

Sincerely,

Nervous Networker

Dear Nervous Networker:

There's no need to be nervous about an informational interview. Just think about it as having a conversation about the industry that you want to be a part of – a topic that should interest both of you. Plus, people love talking about themselves, so focus the conversation on the person, his or her position, and what he or she did to get to that position.

Here are some general tips that should help you make the most of the meeting:

- Show up for your meeting on time or five minutes early. NEVER arrive late. (Make sure you have your contact's cell phone number if an unexpected delay does occur.)
- If you are meeting at a coffee shop or café, you should buy the person's coffee or lunch to show your appreciation.

- Don't expect the person you are meeting with to carry the conversation. Research the person and his or her company and develop a list of questions that you can refer to during the interview.
- Ask for recommendations of who else you should talk to.
- Bring your resume in case the person asks to see it.
- Respect the person's time and keep the meeting to the length you requested.
- Always follow up with a thank-you note. (See page 56 for tips on writing a thank-you note.)

Making networking less intimidating

Dear Ann E. Answers:

I'm a young professional who is looking to expand my professional network. Being part of the tech-savvy generation, I've become so attuned to online networking through e-mail, Twitter and LinkedIn that the idea of being in a room full of professionals at a meet-and-greet seems incredibly daunting. How can I change my mind-set to make in-person networking less intimidating?

Sincerely,

Muddled Mingler

Dear Muddled Mingler:

Stop hiding behind technology. Yes, technology is wonderful. But it should complement in-person networking, not replace it. There is a big difference between virtual rapport and in-person chemistry.

Do you like to go to social functions with your friends? Think of "networking" as a fancy synonym for "socializing." Suddenly networking events become business parties. Thinking along these lines can eliminate the pressure and stress associated with memorizing an elevator speech, worrying about what you're wearing, and approaching intimidating professionals.

Remember that everyone in attendance is there for the same reasons: to meet people and hopefully cultivate mutually beneficial business relationships.

The best way to prepare for this type of social affair is to know what you have to offer, be able to articulately present it in conversation, and be willing to make the first move to introduce yourself.

But if this advice alone doesn't help you overcome your inhibitions, just remind yourself: with practice comes confidence. Do it once, critique yourself, learn from your mistakes, and repeat.

Nothing about networking has to be daunting with the right attitude. After all, wouldn't you like to put a face and/or personality to a company or brand – especially if you are going to pursue a business relationship with that person or organization? Plus, you can always follow up with your new contacts using technology such as e-mail or LinkedIn.

According to the U.S. Bureau of Labor Statistics, 70% of jobs are found through networking. Since many job positions are filled by word-of-mouth referrals, it is important to not just consider who you know, but who knows you, too.

U.S. Bureau of Labor Statistics, "Job Openings and Labor Turnover Survey," (May 2012).

Update Status

Engaging in a hyper-connected world

Is there such a thing as social media overload?

Dear Ann E. Answers:

My friends call me a social media junkie, because every time a new social media tool is introduced, I want to try it. I don't think I'm out of the ordinary (though sometimes it does seem like a chore). Is there such a thing as too much social media?

Sincerely,

Social Media Obsessed

Dear Social Media Obsessed:
Depending on your personal and professional goals – whether they are networking, meeting new friends, learning something new, engaging in discussion, or exchanging information – using a variety of social media tools may or may not help you reach them.

Many people today think it's cool to be an early adopter of social media channels, but it is important to have a valid reason behind your decision to participate in a new social medium. In other words, don't get a Twitter account if you don't plan on using it. But if you want to learn more about a new trend, try it. The best way to understand the tool and the benefits it offers is to explore it.

Before biting off more than you can chew, evaluate the social media tool, decide how it could benefit you, and – if you join – make a commitment to stay active and engaged for at least a month or two. A social media presence is only as valuable as the amount of effort put into it. If you eventually decide the program isn't useful or beneficial, delete your account. Having inactive social media accounts can actually harm your online reputation. Social media requires conversing with your customers; neglecting social media accounts may send the message that you don't value the people following your business.

Only 47% of Twitter accounts are active, and half of the registered Twitter users follow two or fewer people. Approximately 11% of Facebook accounts are inactive.

Mindjumpers, "The Sharing Avalanche," (2011).

The importance of a LinkedIn profile

Dear Ann E. Answers:

I have never used LinkedIn before, but I often get e-mails from business acquaintances asking to connect on the site. Do you think I should join? If so, what should I put in my profile?

Sincerely,

LinkedIn Newbie

Dear LinkedIn Newbie:

The real question is why you aren't on LinkedIn in the first place. Yes, you should absolutely set up a LinkedIn profile. While social networks like Facebook are too personal for professional relationships, LinkedIn is the ideal platform for sharing credentials and networking with other professionals online.

While millions of people have LinkedIn profiles, very few people take full advantage of the opportunities that LinkedIn provides. Essentially, LinkedIn is a free space to post information about your professional experience. Your LinkedIn profile should act as a polished, online resume. Make sure you include information about current and past positions, education, professional affiliations, and volunteer activities. Having an incomplete profile can hinder your online image.

Your profile can also include endorsements and/or recommendations from other LinkedIn users about your work habits and personality traits. These testimonials will enhance your credibility, because it always looks better when someone else boasts about your skills.

You should also consider joining LinkedIn groups related to your professional field. This is a great way to connect with new people who have similar interests and skills. You never know; you might learn something from them.

Once you're satisfied with your page, you should publicize it on your other social media networks, or even include the LinkedIn icon in your e-mail signature.

> LinkedIn has more than 200 million users, 37% of whom live in the United States. Approximately two new members join LinkedIn every second.
>
> *TechCrunch*, "LinkedIn Hits 200 Million Registered Users Worldwide," (January 9, 2013).

Boundaries for social media connections

Dear Ann E. Answers:

I recently connected with one of my clients on LinkedIn, and I followed it up with a Facebook friend request. It has been a week and the friendship has yet to be accepted. I'm starting to wonder if I crossed the line.

Sincerely,

Potential Boundary Crosser

Dear Potential Boundary Crosser:
I hate to be the bearer of bad news, but yes, you crossed the line. Just look at the taglines for LinkedIn and Facebook and you'll know why. LinkedIn is the "world's largest professional network," while Facebook is "the social network."

Do not become Facebook friends with someone unless you are friends with them in real life. I'm not sure why some people don't follow this simple guideline, especially when you consider all of the personal information that can be found on Facebook. If you were a financial planner, would you want your clients to know how you spend your money on the weekends? I certainly wouldn't. The best approach is to not become Facebook friends with a professional acquaintance unless the relationship morphs into a genuine friendship.

On the other hand, LinkedIn is a great venue to network professionally and reinforce business connections, but you should not connect with someone on LinkedIn unless you have met them before, or, at the very least, talked on the phone or exchanged e-mails in a professional setting.

If you had boundary problems with Facebook and LinkedIn, you also might wonder when it's appropriate to follow people on Twitter. Twitter's tagline is "follow your interests," so you can follow pretty much anyone you want. It's the only social media site I know of where it's not necessarily creepy to follow a stranger. That's because the person doesn't have to follow you back. Additionally, personal information is limited on Twitter. It is meant for sharing information in real time, though in my opinion not for learning what someone had for breakfast.

Don't worry about past friend requests that haven't been accepted. Most people are flattered by the request, even if they don't accept. Just think about the type of relationships you have before you make future friend requests.

Should I link social media accounts?

Dear Ann E. Answers:

When my company created accounts on Facebook and Twitter, we were overwhelmed by the amount of time it took to keep the accounts populated. So we decided to link our accounts so that anything we post on Facebook will be posted on Twitter and vice versa. But recently we've started to get complaints from our customers who find it confusing or annoying to read posts meant for Twitter on the Facebook page. Some of them have even "unliked" our page because of it! Should we unlink our social media accounts?

Sincerely,

Over-Linked

Dear Over-Linked:

In the early days of social media, a lot of companies fell into the same trap that your company has fallen into. They linked their social media accounts so that it would be easier to maintain a regular presence on them. It seemed like an efficient choice at the time, but any company that still links its accounts risks losing followers.

This is not a smart move, as you have found out with your dissatisfied customers. Each social media channel has unique qualities that attract a specific type of audience – some like Twitter's real-time nature, while others prefer the ability to share longer posts on Facebook. Because each social media site has its own niche, it's important to interact with your followers in the style promoted by each site. Excessive or confusing posts from Twitter could alienate your Facebook fans and cause them to disregard future posts.

The same could be true for Facebook posts that are automatically posted to Twitter. Rather than linking your accounts, you should post separate messages on each. The messages should be similar, but each message should reflect your recognition that different audiences deserve to receive information the way that they want it. Don't roll your eyes at me – this will only take an extra five minutes of your day. Unlink your accounts now before you lose any more customers.

Social media addictions

Dear Ann E. Answers:

My husband recently got a smartphone and loves using it to update his Twitter account. He always tweets about which important business people he had lunch with, and he even brings it out at the dinner table to tweet about the conversation we're having. Am I just jealous of my husband's new love, or has he become addicted to his smartphone and social media?

Sincerely,

Ready to Intervene

Dear Ready to Intervene:

Your husband seems to be struggling with social media addiction. It's time you intervene before he commits any more social media faux pas!

First of all, he needs to place more value on the here and now. If he is spending time with close friends and family in a small setting, like dinner, it's not appropriate to tweet about it.

Tweeting about lunch dates publicly is not an authentic form of communication, especially if he is trying to thank the person for meeting with him. In fact, it goes beyond networking and borders on narcissism. Blatant name-dropping devalues relationships and can put authentic, one-on-one connections at risk. Instead, he should send a direct message to thank his lunch companion.

However, publicizing panel engagements, promotions, or client news via Twitter is appropriate in limited quantities. He should ask himself who he wants to read the post. If the message is meant for friends, colleagues, or the business community, post it publicly. But if the message is a personal thank-you for the person's time, don't tweet it publicly.

Are you a social media addict?

1. Do you check social media sites before you roll out of bed in the morning?
   ☐ Yes
   ☐ No

2. If you're in a public place by yourself, do you look at social media sites on your smartphone so you don't feel so lonely?
   ☐ Yes
   ☐ No

3. Have you ever texted, e-mailed, or tweeted while driving?
   ☐ Yes
   ☐ No

4. If your smartphone rings or vibrates in the middle of personal business, have you ever taken your phone out to see what the message is?
   ☐ Yes
   ☐ No

5. Have you ever posted to someone's Facebook wall while you were in the same room with that person?
   ☐ Yes
   ☐ No

6. Do you "check in" to every place you go?
   - ☐ Yes
   - ☐ No

7. Have you ever checked a social media site so frequently that you notice that there aren't any new posts?
   - ☐ Yes
   - ☐ No

8. Do you prefer to coordinate social gatherings via Facebook or Twitter instead of through phone calls or texts?
   - ☐ Yes
   - ☐ No

9. Do you find yourself subconsciously thinking of witty hashtags for future tweets?
   - ☐ Yes
   - ☐ No

If you check six yes boxes, you are indeed a social media addict.

What is the value of a Twitter follower?

Dear Ann E. Answers:

I am the director of social media at my company. Whenever expenses get scrutinized, the value of our company's Twitter account is questioned. While I have no difficulties educating "the suits" about Twitter's strategic value, even I have trouble explaining it in dollars and cents. What is the monetary value of a Twitter account?

Sincerely,

Will Tweet for Cash

Dear Will Tweet for Cash:

It seems like someone somewhere is finding a way to monetize just about everything. Case in point, divorce courts have been putting a price on love for decades. When it comes to social media, services like Klout try to measure its value in terms of influence, but monetizing a Twitter follower is – and always will be – an inexact science.

That's not to say people haven't tried to estimate the value of Twitter. The first real attempt came in 2011, when technology website PhoneDog.com sued one of its former employees. The company claimed that Noah Kravitz improperly used his Twitter handle – which he had developed on company time – after he left the company and, therefore, owed PhoneDog $2.50 per Twitter follower per month. So, in this case, PhoneDog believes each Twitter follower is worth $30 per year.

Using this formula, a company's Twitter handle with 300,000 followers is worth $9 million a year.

With spammers and abandoned accounts making up a good chunk of the Twitterverse, it's safe to say that not all followers are worth $2.50 a month. But perhaps some of the most active Twitter users are worth even more than that. There will never be a universally accepted value of a Twitter follower, but I guarantee this won't be the last attempt to put a price on a follower. The one value of Twitter that people can't ignore is the real-time customer engagement it provides to companies. That, to me, is priceless.

TweetValue, a service powered by Twitter, assigns a dollar value to Twitter profiles. According to the site, "the value is calculated with a Ph.D. algorithm that is based on the public information available on your Twitter profile." As of this writing, Justin Bieber had the highest all-time TweetValue, listed at $169,444.

TweetValue, *"How Much Is Your Twitter Profile Worth?"* (February 13, 2013).

Define your Twitter persona

Dear Ann E. Answers:

I have a personal Twitter account. I wasn't asked to join for work purposes, but I list my employer in my bio. My company hasn't given me guidelines on what constitutes a work-appropriate tweet. Should I steer clear of social or non-work-related tweets if I disclose my employer in my Twitter profile?

Sincerely,

Separation of Work and Play

Dear Separation of Work and Play:

When you join Twitter, you should decide whether your tweets will be professional or personal. Although you've pursued the professional route by attaching your employer to your Twitter identity, you can still show your personality in your tweets, especially if it is in good taste and complies with your company policy.

First, ask if your company has a social media policy, or put a disclaimer in your bio stating: "My tweets are my own."

Whatever your motivation is to be on Twitter, don't make your tweets one-dimensional. In other words, if you are constantly tweeting about your industry or your clients, your followers will think of you as more of a brand robot than an actual person with opinions and interests.

It's okay to discuss your interests, participate in conversations, and express your opinions – as long as you aren't bad-mouthing others. Tweeting about a great blog you read, a new restaurant you tried, or a question you have on your mind are all appropriate ways to add a personal touch to your Twitter identity, engage with others, and build a diverse following.

However, when you are on company time, be mindful of the time you spend posting non-work-related tweets. You don't want to give the impression to clients and colleagues that you are neglecting your work just to banter about the latest celebrity gossip.

#MTAMO (My Tweets Are My Own) is a universally recognized hashtag that can be used in a Twitter bio or when posting tweets that express personal content. But human resources experts tell me this does not cover you legally. If you write anything bad about your company on Twitter, you may face consequences, regardless of whether you use the #MTAMO hashtag.

Blog tips

Dear Ann E. Answers:

Until recently my attitude toward blogs was unenthusiastic at best. I wondered why people would care about what I think. But I have come to realize that blogs are more than just a platform where egomaniacs give their two cents. I'm thinking about starting my own blog, and I want to do it the right way. Do you have any tips?

Sincerely,

Blog Newbie

Dear Blog Newbie:

You asked the golden question that everyone should ask when starting a blog. Why should people care about what you think? The best blogs are ones that focus on a topic and are not just "anything goes" blogs. If you treat your blog like a personal journal and write about whatever pops into your head, chances are the only people who will read it will be your family and close friends (if that).

Conversely, you should view your blog as a valuable career development tool. Blogging is a great way to market yourself and share your expertise. When deciding on the focus of your blog, think about your career field and areas of expertise. Once you have decided on a blog topic, choose a memorable name and create your blog. This can be done for free and only takes a couple of hours. The most popular software programs for this are WordPress, TypePad and Blogger.

Next is the hardest part. Once you have created your blog, you must commit to posting regularly. Start slowly.

You don't necessarily need to post every day, let alone multiple times each day. Set a reasonable frequency goal – one or two entries per week at a minimum. This way you have time to brainstorm relevant topics and write high-quality entries.

Blogging is all about quality over quantity. Studies have shown that up to 95% of blogs are abandoned. If you have something worthwhile to share, don't let your blog become part of that statistic.

In 2009, the *Wall Street Journal* dubbed blogging "America's newest profession," citing that there are now more paid bloggers in the United States than there are firefighters or computer programmers.

Mark Penn, *"America's Newest Profession: Bloggers for Hire," Wall Street Journal, (April 21, 2009).*

Constructive online commenting

Dear Ann E. Answers:

When reading news articles online, I am sometimes inspired to post my reaction in the reader comment section below the article. However, I am often turned off by some of the controversial remarks posted anonymously in the comment section. Is it worthwhile to join the comment conversation, or should I avoid stooping to that level?

Sincerely,

Quietly Opinionated

Dear Quietly Opinionated:

When reader comment sections were first unveiled, I thought it was a First Amendment breakthrough. But when I read some of the controversial anonymous postings you speak of, I quickly swore them off. And I'm glad I did.

I think it's important that we read news articles for informational purposes and form our own opinions and reactions to news stories without being swayed by remarks from other readers. That said, reader comment sections are a part of our culture; most media outlets probably won't disable them anytime soon, because they are legal and can help drive web traffic.

Should you feel inclined to comment on news articles, here are some ground rules:

- **Do not respond immediately**. If the article or its subsequent comments trigger an emotional reaction, wait at least 30 minutes before posting your comment. Emotional posts usually end in regret.

- **Use your real name.** Own up to what you say and be prepared to defend it.
- **Be accurate.** It is okay to make emotionally charged comments, but don't let your emotions get in the way of being truthful.
- **Be tasteful.** Remember where you come from and who you represent. What if your employer reads your comment? Even more, what would your mother think?
- **Do not personally attack other people.** Even if other readers are attacking you, take the high road. Be better than that.

You need to apply a filter of appropriate skepticism when reading comments, just as news consumers should apply a filter to news stories. Intelligent and productive conversations do take place in reader comment sections. Unfortunately, these productive conversations are often overshadowed by a cesspool of anonymous – and sometimes heinous – blabber.

"Transparency and reasoned debate are crucial parts of the web culture, and it's a disappointment to us that we have not been able to maintain a civil conversation, especially about issues that people feel strongly (and differently) about."

– *Jim Brady, former executive editor of WashingtonPost.com, after shutting down the comment section of the Washington Post blog*

Viral videos in good taste

Dear Ann E. Answers:

My company has been using television commercials as our main advertising tool for decades, but we question if it's as effective as it used to be. We're exploring the idea of creating a viral video for our next advertisement. Do you have any advice on how we can make our next commercial a YouTube sensation?

Sincerely,

Going Viral

Dear Going Viral:

So you're jealous of the "shirtless Old Spice guy" campaign? I don't blame you. Those commercials enjoyed hundreds of millions of online views, which helped position Old Spice as a relevant and trendy brand. With the right viral video, your brand can enjoy the same widespread attention.

The most important step toward going viral is producing a creative product that will grab people's attention. But how do you get people's attention? There's no right answer to this question, but I can tell you that the most successful viral videos are creative, humorous and short (between 30 and 60 seconds). Also, throw the formula you've been using for TV commercials out the window. Most people do not want to watch commercials online, so the most popular viral videos for brands do not *seem* like advertisements. Viral videos are more likely to resonate with viewers when they do not focus on the benefits of a product or service.

Viral videos do not have to be high in quality or cost. Content is most important. This is why I suggest focusing your efforts and resources on the creative brainstorming process and coming up with a new, creative idea. Flash mobs became a YouTube sensation in 2010. Planking was the hot fad of 2011, followed by the Harlem Shake in 2012. What innovative concept can you introduce this year?

Once the video is created, share it without limits or shame. E-mail it to everyone you know. Post it on every video-sharing website you can find (not just YouTube). Share it on all of the social media sites you can find (not just Facebook and Twitter) and seek feedback from your target audience. Constructive criticism will make your next video even better. Embed the video on your company blog, and accompany it with an entry about the making of the video. If it doesn't take off right away, be patient for a few days. Some things take awhile to catch on, even in the fast-paced online world we live in. If your first video doesn't go viral, don't give up. It's difficult to predict which videos will become the next big thing.

Before you go ahead and decide to produce an online video, let me offer a word of caution: Don't just produce a video for the sake of doing a video. Strategy is very important. Be prepared to discuss and make a case for why a video makes sense in a particular situation. Also, make sure your video is tasteful. With the fast-paced sharing that takes place online, offensive ad campaigns can backfire in a matter of minutes.

Refresh

Vintage communications to
impress a modern audience

The importance of thank-you notes

Dear Ann E. Answers:

I was recently laid off and am hunting for a job. Besides responding to job postings, I have been attending local networking events and initiating informational interviews with business professionals in my field. It seems like I am on the right track toward finding a job, but I'm unsure about the appropriate way to thank someone for meeting with me. Is a verbal "thanks" at the end of our meeting enough, or do I need to send an e-mail, handwritten note, or something else?

Sincerely,

Gracious Job Seeker

Dear Gracious Job Seeker:

Verbal thanks is not enough. There is no such thing as being too thankful, and the most authentic way to convey your appreciation is through a handwritten thank-you note. Who doesn't love to get a card in the mail – especially one that is praising you for your grace?

As a rule, you should send an e-mail of appreciation on the same day you meet with the person. The message can be brief, and then you can elaborate on your gratitude in the handwritten note. No matter what, your choice of words is what truly matters.

The message should include:

- A genuine thanks to the person for his/her time
- A reference to something specific that was talked about in the interview or meeting to help this person remember you

- A reiteration of your interest in the industry, company, or specific position and why you would be a good fit
- A closing that both welcomes further contact and – if it is in regard to a job interview – expresses your interest in receiving his/her final decision

As a reminder, if you meet with multiple people, be sure to send a note of thanks to each person. Professionals will appreciate that you went the extra mile to personalize your notes.

Getting in the habit of writing thank-you notes can only help your chances of landing a job. A survey by CareerBuilder.com found that nearly 22% of hiring managers would be less likely to hire a job candidate who neglected to send a thank-you note after an interview. One of my favorite thank-you note resources is the Mannersmith Thank You Note Wizard at mannersmith.com.

CareerBuilder.com, "More Than One in Five Hiring Managers Say They Are Less Likely to Hire a Candidate Who Didn't Send a Thank-You Note, Finds New CareerBuilder Survey," (April 14, 2011).

Is cursive relevant today?

Dear Ann E. Answers:

Some schools are abandoning the teaching of cursive and pushing keyboarding skills instead. But I guess I'm old-school enough to still use cursive in things like handwritten thank-you notes. Will I appear like a fuddy-duddy in today's business world if I keep this up?

Sincerely,

Old-Fashioned Writer

Dear Old-Fashioned Writer:
Thoughtful words penned in ink just don't have the same impact when typed out.

Setting the right tone happens not only through the words we choose, but also through how we choose to convey them. Handwritten notes in cursive – or, at the very least, neat printing – are still the best way to personally and professionally say: "I care enough about the courtesy you extended to send you a note that I wrote myself."

When I write a handwritten note, I find myself carefully selecting every word – because I know that I can't neatly cross something out or move sentences and paragraphs around as I can on the computer. In some mystifying way, using cursive implies an even higher level of importance and thoughtful care. No new technology can make that claim.

When should I cite my sources?

Dear Ann E. Answers:

I do a lot of writing at work, and sometimes I use statistics to back up my arguments. I don't generally cite my sources because footnotes seem too academic. Am I plagiarizing?

Sincerely,

Closet Plagiarist

Dear Closet Plagiarist:

Yes. Did your college professors not beat into your head the importance of giving other authors proper credit for their work?

More importantly, citations legitimize the information presented in your written work. By attributing facts and statistics to their original authors, you make it possible for readers to view the original sources to double-check the statistics or learn more about a topic. Your credibility will be enhanced as a result.

Depending on the type of writing you do, footnotes aren't always necessary. You could use an in-text citation ("According to the Pew Research Center . . ."). Rather than bog down a sentence with excessive wordiness, these simple citation phrases actually help each sentence flow into the next. You could also provide a link to the report or study if you are writing website copy or a blog post.

Your ultimate goal is to reach your audience through strong, compelling arguments. When you make claims, be sure you back them up with facts so that your messages aren't compromised by doubt.

Print marketing tips

Dear Ann E. Answers:

My company is putting together a new communications plan. Some people believe printed pieces are "old-school" and a waste of money. What do you think? Are printed communications still relevant today?

Sincerely,

Puzzled Printer

Dear Puzzled Printer:

It is no surprise that the print world claims a smaller piece of the marketing pie than it once did. With smaller budgets, less time, and the overwhelming number of people found online, businesses use e-mail, social media, and mobile marketing more frequently than offline mediums to reach their audiences.

However, there are still audiences who prefer to get the written word offline and times when print is better. The key is to match the occasion and message with the appropriate communications vehicle. For example, if you're planning a high school reunion, Facebook might be the most effective means to reach the majority of your audience. But for an open house or awards presentation, a printed piece is appropriate.

Consider who you are trying to reach. Even people who consume most of their information online still value a printed piece of marketing collateral. If your company's printed pieces are well-designed, include compelling content, and are consistent with your online brand, they will be perceived as trustworthy and can add credibility to your brand.

Depending on your campaign and audience, print and online marketing can work together for your business, just as these efforts might also work with broadcast or print advertising and telemarketing. If you choose to do this, it is important to include your online information in your print materials, such as your website URL, e-mail address, and icons for any social media accounts your company has. Then post a PDF file of the document on your website and social media sites.

You could also print a QR (Quick Response) code on your collateral, whether it is a brochure, newsletter, flyer, or business card. QR codes are a great way to integrate print and digital marketing efforts and serve as a valid measurement tool to help you determine the success of your print marketing campaign. Last time I checked, QR codes are far from being "old-school."

Tips to boost event RSVPs

Dear Ann E. Answers:

It seems as though I have been dubbed the "event planner" among my family, friends and coworkers. That's okay except that my biggest pet peeve about this assumed role is when people neglect to RSVP. Isn't there a rule for providing RSVPs? And, does the type of invitation matter when it comes to RSVP expectations?

Sincerely,

Peeved Planner

Dear Peeved Planner:

There is nothing more irritating than when your event planning comes to a halt because you are waiting for people to RSVP.

Unfortunately, there isn't a universal code of conduct, because it depends on the event. Nevertheless, RSVP is an abbreviation for the French phrase "Répondez, s'il vous plait," which literally means "please respond." Therefore, invitees should always be courteous and respond promptly, even if the response is a "no." Most formal invites will include an RSVP deadline, which can help to urge a timely response.

When it comes to planning a formal event, select an RSVP date that is one week earlier than your absolute final deadline, to allow yourself time for any last-minute responses or follow-up phone calls. That being said, the length of time between sending the invitation and the actual event also factors into the response rate.

Planning too far in advance might result in lost invites and forgotten responses, but sending out invitations too close to the event might draw a low turnout rate. Unless it is a wedding or an event of equal status where there is a specific set of rules, sending an invitation six weeks in advance and asking for RSVPs two weeks before the event date should be sufficient.

Also, the choice of invitation mode *does* matter. Your invitation should match the formality of your event. If you decide to go with an e-mail invite, it never hurts to send a friendly reminder to the people who haven't responded as the RSVP deadline approaches. After all, we all know that inboxes get flooded and e-mails get lost.

You should save Facebook invites for informal social gatherings where a final headcount is less important. Otherwise, add a disclaimer that states "a maybe will be counted as a no." "Maybe" is not a definitive answer, nor can it accurately predict if it will turn into a "yes" or a "no."

There is almost always someone who either forgets to respond to an RSVP or mixes up the date or time. Try not to let it ruin your party.

Two of the biggest reasons people neglect to RSVP is because they either forget or don't understand the meaning of "RSVP." Other ways to phrase the French acronym are "Regrets only" or "Please respond by [said date]." I urge you to not rely on "regrets only," because people who do not plan to attend an event are less likely to inform the event organizer.

The practice of asking for a response to an invitation has been around at least since the time of the court of King Louis XIV of France.

Write Once, Revise Twice

Creating meaningful content

The importance of proofreading

Dear Ann E. Answers:

I write e-mails nonstop at work. I am in such a rush that I rarely reread what I have written, but a coworker recently pointed out a dumb grammatical error in an e-mail I had sent her. I felt like such an idiot, but I often don't have time to do more than dash off a quick message. Since this is the first time I've heard about an error in my writing, should I really spend time proofreading every e-mail?

Sincerely,

Writing Whiz

Dear Writing Whiz:
Just because your coworker is the first person to inform you of a mistake doesn't mean that your other e-mails have been error-free.

People will often rely on their computer's spell check or grammar check to catch any writing mistakes, but these software tools are not perfect. Relying solely on them, rather than also using your eyes and your brain, will lead to mistakes. For example, if you intend to write "from" but accidently type "form," these programs will not catch your mistake. Both words are spelled correctly, but depending on the context, one of them would definitely be incorrect.

Even though proofreading takes extra time, doing so will save you embarrassment and make a better impression on others. Not to mention, proofreading can make you a better editor, writer, and even speaker of the English language.

Try printing out your e-mails and proofing them on paper instead of a computer screen, or read your e-mails out loud. Besides catching grammatical errors, a proofread can help you catch awkwardly worded phrases that could be misinterpreted by the recipient, which eliminates the time needed to send follow-up e-mails.

Otherwise, you can always ask another coworker to proof your e-mails. Sometimes you can be too close to the writing and may need a fresh set of eyes to double-check your work. Regardless, proofreading is time well spent.

> Your/you're, its/it's, there/their, and affect/effect are commonly transposed – yet correctly spelled – words.

Overusing clichés

Dear Ann E. Answers:

I have a coworker who is notorious for using clichés in her e-mails and memos. You'd be hard-pressed to not find phrases like "hit the ground running" or "think outside the box" in her everyday writing. For someone who advises others to think outside the box, you'd think she would take her own advice and be more creative with her words. Do you have any advice on how to "steer her clear" of this annoying habit?

Sincerely,

Cease Clichés

Dear Cease Clichés:

In certain situations, cliché expressions can be the best way to phrase a thought. Used sparingly, clichés can lighten the mood and make a point that both sides understand.

However, used often, cliché statements imply inexperience or unoriginality instead of casual puns or wit. Creativity in word selection can be more impactful to the reader than overused phrases that get overlooked. In other words, instead of saying "let's hit the ground running," an original or simpler form of that phrase, such as "let's get started," would be more effective.

Finding alternatives for clichés is not rocket science. It's time for the moment of truth: Tell your coworker the writing is on the wall that her use of clichés needs to stop, or you'll give her a taste of her own medicine.

She can either push her luck and use them, or avoid them like the plague. Again, it isn't rocket science.

Each year Michigan's Lake Superior State University releases an annual list of words deemed so overused that they should be banished. A few notable words and phrases that have made the list include "24/7," "amazing," "thanks in advance," "ginormous," and "win the future."

Lake Superior State University, *Banished Words List*, (2012).

Understanding acronyms

Dear Ann E. Answers:

Lately I have been really annoyed by acronyms. It seems like every meeting I am in I get lost in a sea of letters that stand for words that I quickly forget. Are there rules about acronyms that should be followed during meetings?

Sincerely,

Annoyed by Acronyms

Dear Annoyed by Acronyms:

In my opinion the world would be a better place if fewer acronyms existed. Although no universal guidelines govern the creation of acronyms, below are some general rules to follow.

When using an acronym either orally or in writing, the full name should be stated at least once before switching to the acronym form. For example, on first reference, refer to the Department of Natural Resources, not the "DNR." However, for casual acronyms that are universally understood and used in less formal situations, there can be exceptions to this rule. For example, "ASAP" and "FYI" do not need to be spelled out. And, of course, this rule can be bent or broken depending on your audience.

Before creating an acronym, ask yourself if it is necessary. If the full name to be replaced by the acronym is not very long, chances are that an acronym is unnecessary.

The shorter the acronym, the better. One of the easiest ways to avoid lengthy acronyms is to omit acronym letters for words like "and" or "of" that are part of the long title. For example, the Public Relations Society of America is abbreviated PRSA instead of PRSOA. Exceptions can be made when the vowel helps the acronym form an easily pronounced word (e.g., Department of Transportation or "DOT").

In general, acronyms that include five or fewer letters are best, unless it can be said as a word for short, such as NABET, instead of N-A-B-E-T (which refers to the National Association of Broadcast Employees and Technicians).

Lastly, use good judgment. Just because your preschool organization is called Kindly Keeping Kids does not mean you should abbreviate with the acronym "KKK."

May I end a sentence with a preposition?

Dear Ann E. Answers:

I was taught never to end a sentence with a preposition. It is one of my biggest pet peeves when I see it in writing, especially in a formal document or article. Am I being too formal? Do prepositions really need to remain in the beginning or middle of sentences?

Sincerely,

Preposition Enforcer

Dear Preposition Enforcer:
I regularly write sentences that end with prepositions – words like "in" and "for," which many of us remember being told never to end a sentence with.

Call me a rule breaker, but ending a sentence with a preposition is not grammatically incorrect. According to many grammar style guides, writers should use common sense in deciding whether or not to end a sentence with a preposition. Moreover, the grammarians who devised this rule are ignoring historical linguistic usage. (Look up "German separable prefix" sometime.)

Whenever it makes sense, I recommend reworking a sentence to avoid ending it with a preposition. For example, use "He took the car in which I was riding" instead of "He took the car I was riding in." But if doing so makes the sentence seem awkward or archaic, it is okay to keep the preposition at the end of the sentence.

My advice to you is to lighten up on preposition enforcement. The world is full of grammatical slights that are much more serious than this one.

> Sir Winston Churchill left us with some common sense on the subject of ending sentences with prepositions. In 1948, an editor supposedly reworked one of Churchill's sentences to avoid ending it with a preposition. Churchill replied, "This is the sort of bloody nonsense up with which I will not put."
>
> **Sir Ernest Gowers, *Plain Word*, (1954).**

Excessive exclamation points

Dear Ann E. Answers:

I recently received the following e-mail from a business acquaintance:

> It was so great to see you at last night's business mixer!!! I enjoyed learning more about you and your company, and I can't wait to see you at the next event!!!!

We did make a great business connection at the event, and she seemed very professional, but the excessive exclamation points in her follow-up e-mail gave me the opposite impression. What are the rules about using exclamation points?

Sincerely,

Over-Exclaimed

Dear Over-Exclaimed:

Exclamation points are often used as a crutch when a writer feels the language is not powerful enough to convey the message. People also fall into using exclamation points to show approval of other people or try to appear more interested in the conversation.

Unfortunately, using more than one exclamation point at the end of a sentence may be perceived as a lack of professionalism and can be off-putting to the reader. You will make your point more effectively through better word choice than excessive exclamation points.

In fact, overusing exclamation points ruins the effectiveness of using them at all. For example, when you get angry with someone, raising your voice is only effective if used in limited situations. The same is true with exclamation points.

If you stick to using one exclamation point per paragraph, perhaps the over-exclaimers will get wise to their bad habit and cut down on their hyperactive use of that key on their keyboards.

In the newspaper industry, a headline with an exclamation point is often called a screamer, gasper or startler. Because exclamation points are rarely used in headlines, they really grab the reader's attention.

National Punctuation Day, September 24, is the official day to celebrate commas, colons, semicolons, and other punctuation marks that grace the English language.

Are emoticons ever appropriate in business?

Dear Ann E. Answers:

I am a sarcastic person. I often use emoticons ☺ to express jest and other emotions when e-mailing or texting my friends, but someone frowned on my using them in business e-mails. I'm confused and don't know if I should be using emoticons ☹.

Sincerely,

Emoticon Lover ❤

Dear Emoticon Lover:
Why are you being sarcastic in business communications? You're probably not getting paid to crack jokes. (If you're a comedian, I apologize.) There is a time and a place for sarcasm, and it's generally not in an e-mail to a client. The same is true for sharing other emotions, such as disappointment ☹, happiness ☺, or confusion ☺.

You should evaluate the relationships that you have with your clients and colleagues to determine if it is appropriate to use emoticons in e-mails. Do you have a friendly relationship with your clients? Have you been sarcastic with them in person? Can you portray a friendly or sarcastic tone without emoticons?

In general, it is more appropriate to use emoticons with your colleagues, especially if you are friends. I would err on the side of caution when using emotions with clients. The last thing you want to do is to damage a client relationship by being too informal.

Scott Fahlman, a computer scientist at Carnegie Mellon University, is credited with using the first emoticon in September 1982. Today he gives an annual "Smiley Award" to students who demonstrate excellence in technology-assisted person-to-person communication.

Carnegie Mellon University School of Computer Science, "Smiley Award," www.cs.cmu.edu/smiley/sa.html.

Decoding fonts

Dear Ann E. Answers:

My new business is developing a logo, website, brochure, and other materials. My colleagues and I disagree about what font we should use on these items. While I think Times New Roman is a classic font that reflects the professional nature of our company, my colleagues say Arial is softer. Does a font really say something about a company? And, if so, which font is better, Times New Roman or Arial?

Sincerely,

Times New Roman Faithful

Dear Times New Roman Faithful:

A font is much more than just print characters. To many readers, a company's font choice directly correlates to their perception of the company's culture, professionalism and stability. Typeface can influence whether people perceive e-mails or marketing materials as professional or casual – and if they even decide to read them.

Think of font as a subtle form of propaganda. A letter's density, curve and placement can convey tone, spirit or mood. For example, Marlboro uses thick fonts in its logo to convey manliness, while CoverGirl uses a light, thin font to convey its "easy, breezy" tagline.

While Times New Roman is a staple for formal memos, designed pieces (e.g., logos, websites and brochures) tend to favor more casual sans serif fonts, such as Arial. Typeface is a graphic element. Once you choose a font, stick with it throughout your materials. This will help your company maintain a cohesive graphic identity that is more recognizable to the public.

As for your second question, at least your colleagues aren't pushing for ⬛⬛⬛⬛⬛⬛⬛ or something equally illegible. Times New Roman and Arial are two safe fonts, especially for business communications. But there are dozens of other business-appropriate fonts that could be included in your conversation. Since there is a lot at stake, I recommend hiring a graphic designer to help you determine which fonts will best portray your company's personality.

Tens of thousands of typefaces are available, and each font has a different connotation. Here are a few examples:

Serif fonts have rounded edges on the letters.

- Times New Roman conveys a professional, formal and mature attitude
- Courier is deemed as rigid, dull and unattractive, and should rarely be used

Sans serif fonts do not have any embellishments.

- Arial portrays stability, but it can also be judged as unimaginative. It's best suited for spreadsheets and PowerPoint headlines.
- Comic Sans is often described as youthful and casual, so it's best used for invitations to kids' birthday parties
- **Impact** depicts assertiveness, rigidity and rudeness, plus it is hard to read. It should be used sparingly.

Rebecca Schwartz, "What Your Font Says About You," Reader's Digest, www.readersdigest.ca/home-garden/money/what-your-font-says-about-you.

Text communications

Dear Ann E. Answers:

In light of all the abbreviating, OMGing and LOLing found in the average teenager's texts, will today's teens ever be ready for the real world, where spelling, grammar, and sentence construction matter?

Sincerely,

Worried by Generation Text

Dear Worried by Generation Text:

Language purists, take note. The English language has been vandalized for centuries, and has often been enriched as a result. Texting will most likely lead to an evolution in the English language, but so did the advent of printing and the emigration of Britions to America and elsewhere. Change can be good in healthy doses.

Multiple studies indicate that texting does not harm teenagers' language skills, providing they are also reading books and having verbal conversations with adults. Exposure to and use of language – even through texting – can help kids become more verbally skilled, because they tend to do well at the things they enjoy doing. Likewise, people need to have a good grasp of reading and vocabulary before they can manipulate spellings and create abbreviations. That being said, most of the text abbreviations such as ROFL and BRB are only meant for casual texting conversations, not business communication. However, depending on the business relationship, FYI or ASAP are likely acceptable.

The real challenge may not be with Generation Text's command of the English language, but with their ability to detach from their phones long enough to pay attention to their surroundings and understand when it is and is not appropriate to send text messages.

The average adult, ages 18-24, sends more than 3,200 text messages per month.

Pew Internet and American Life Project, "How Americans Use Text Messaging," (September 19, 2011).

Texting while driving is banned in 39 states and the District of Columbia, while talking on the phone is only banned in 10 states and the District of Columbia.

Governors Highway Safety Association, "Cell Phone and Texting Laws," (February 2013).

Abusing the thesaurus

Dear Ann E. Answers:

I admit it – I often overcompensate for my below-average vernacular by using the thesaurus function in Microsoft Word. Sometimes I insert polysyllabic words that I'm not familiar with if they sound impressive. Is this a bad idea?

Sincerely,

Thesaurus Junkie

Dear Thesaurus Junkie:

When you use words without really knowing their meanings, you might as well be communicating in gibberish. The "slightly wrong" use of words could cause an even bigger problem than your limited vocabulary. If you absolutely must use a thesaurus, I recommend checking out the visual thesaurus (visualthesaurus.com), which differentiates words that are closely related from those that only slightly resemble one another.

Good communicators use big words only when both they and their audiences know the meanings of those words. Written and verbal communications are only effective if people know what you are trying to tell them. Although a large vocabulary is important, your credibility will instantly decrease if you misuse large words. Without taking the time to assess your verbiage, you run the risk of sounding either unintelligent or pretentious.

Too many words – or too many highfalutin words – can actually impede good communication. (That was Hemingway's reason for writing in understated, stripped-down language.)

I offer you this advice: either trade your extra syllables for clarity or start reading the dictionary.

The average American adult reads at an eighth- or ninth-grade level. The New York Times and the Washington Post are written at a tenth-grade reading level.

Plain Language at Work, "What's with the Newspapers?" (2005).

In a letter to a 12-year-old boy, Mark Twain wrote,

"I notice that you use plain, simple language, short words, and brief sentences. That is the way to write English – it is the modern way and the best way. Stick to it, and don't let the fluff and flowers and verbosity creep in. When you catch an adjective, kill it. No I don't mean utterly, but kill most of them – then the rest will be valuable. They weaken when close together. They give strength when they are wide apart."

Samuel Clemens, "Letter to David Watt Bowser" (March 20, 1880).

Tracked changes vs. handwritten edits

Dear Ann E. Answers:

When documents are passed around the office so that several people can comment, should I give my coworkers a paper copy to handwrite their changes on, or e-mail them the document to electronically track their changes? Some people like it one way better than the other, but after trying once to cater to each person's preference, I got confused. What should I do?

Sincerely,

Tracking Sideways

Dear Tracking Sideways:
Sometimes you need to put yourself first. If you are the document's writer and you are at an equal or higher level to the coworkers reviewing the document, you should politely request that everyone do things the same way. Your preference – whether it is handwritten suggestions in red ink or electronically tracked changes – is a courtesy that you deserve to be shown, because you have assumed the bulk of the responsibility.

However, if your supervisor or other higher-ranking coworkers are reviewing the document, provide them the document after others have seen it and ask them if they have a preference for how they make revisions. If they do, respect it. If they don't, freely tell them yours.

Keep in mind that up to this point you have been seeking people's *edits*. But another important step awaits. Your document still needs to be proofread after you make the editing changes. Please, please, PLEASE bring a paper copy to your company's proofreader or to a coworker whose grammar skills you trust. I know from experience (no scientific evidence needed) that some mistakes seem to make it through an on-screen proof that seldom escape a paper proof.

To the greatest extent possible, follow the rules that work best for you to achieve a polished end product. After all, *your* reputation is on the line.

Approve This Message

Mastering the art
of political participation

GOFF
PUBLIC
Relations + Affairs

Communicating with public officials

Dear Ann E. Answers:

There is proposed legislation which could badly impact my livelihood. What's the most effective way to contact a lawmaker, and how can I know that this person will even care about what I have to say?

Sincerely,

Concerned Citizen

Dear Concerned Citizen:
Public officials work for their constituents. Hearing your opinions on issues helps them stay informed and do their job well. The best way to contact most legislators is through a letter, phone call, or e-mail.

There is a misconception that public officials will not receive letters sent via snail mail in a timely fashion, or that the letters will get lost in the mail bin. But, actually, letters written on official letterhead can lend a sense of legitimacy to your concerns. If you are worried about meeting a specific deadline, you could hand-deliver your letter to the lawmaker's office to ensure that he or she receives it on time.

If you call or e-mail a legislator, don't expect a response. Many elected officials have staff members who screen their calls, take messages, and pass them along as appropriate. The same is true with e-mails. More often than not, your e-mail will be read by the legislator's staffer who sorts through the hundreds of e-mails received each day and submits a report to the legislator.

But your message will be heard. Make sure you prepare ahead of time before placing a call so you can be clear and concise in your wording, which is especially important when leaving a voicemail (see page 10).

When you call or e-mail, provide your name and address and indicate if you are a constituent. Then provide the name and file number of the legislation, your stance on the issue, and a thank-you for that person's time. If you support or oppose a bill, explain why and how that bill could impact you – either positively or negatively. But be concise. Keep in mind legislators and their staffers don't have time to read lengthy e-mails, but they will appreciate knowing why you support or oppose a certain bill.

Also, if you are calling the legislator's office, get the name of the person you spoke with for future reference.

Sometimes a coalition or group may ask you to contact your legislators. The group may provide a sample letter for you to send. While it might be easy to just send it as is, personalizing the message will have a greater impact on your legislators.

Also, as a general rule, each issue you are contacting the public official about deserves a separate phone call, letter, or e-mail.

As of 2012, President Barack Obama received more than 65,000 letters every week and about 100,000 e-mails, 1,000 faxes, and 3,000 phone calls per day.

ThisIsHowYouDoIt.com, "How to contact President Obama," (February 12, 2013).

How to address an elected official

Dear Ann E. Answers:

I'm good friends with my city's mayor, so I call him by his first name when we see each other in public. I want to contact him about an issue in our city that I feel strongly about. Should I address him by his first name, like I normally do, or as "Mr. Mayor"?

Sincerely,

Hizzoner's Chum

Dear Hizzoner's Chum:

When talking with elected officials about specific issues, you should always address them in a professional, respectful manner by using their titles, regardless of any personal friendship you might have with them.

If you decide to write a letter or e-mail to your mayor, the address line should read "The Honorable" before his/her full first and last name and the greeting should read "Mayor" followed by the person's last name.

You should address other elected officials – members of Congress, state legislators, etc. – in a similar fashion. Even if you don't like the person who you are addressing, using the proper title as a show of respect is important if you wish to be taken seriously.

Even though it may seem uncomfortable to address a good friend so formally, remember that you are addressing this person in an official capacity about an issue that affects you as a citizen of the town – not as a personal friend.

The mayor also may share letters, e-mails, and other messages from concerned citizens with city council members or staff, making it even more important to communicate seriously and professionally.

For more information about contacting an elected official and what to include in your message, see page 88.

Live-tweeting tips

Dear Ann E. Answers:

I am a journalist/blogger and spend a good chunk of my time covering public hearings. I am active on Twitter and would like to start live-tweeting at some of the hearings, but I have never used Twitter to transmit information in real time. Can you give me some tips for live-tweeting?

Sincerely,

Live on Location

Dear Live on Location:

I think it's great that you are ready to take your relationship with your loyal Twitter followers to the next level. I enjoy following journalists and bloggers who tweet in real time because they do a great service – providing information to interested people who don't have the time or resources to attend every event that affects their lives. However, live-tweeting can be ineffective – and even annoying to followers – if the tweeter doesn't do it correctly. Below is a list of tips to consider as you move forward with your live-tweeting adventure.

1. Create a hashtag

Hashtags are words or phrases prefixed with the symbol #. They enable users to categorize topics and easily find information on Twitter. Select a #hashtag for the event you are covering which is appropriate, concise, and easy to remember. The longer your hashtag is, the fewer characters you have for your actual message. Plus, if the hashtag is too long, you increase the risk of having your followers get it wrong.

2. Notify your followers

This is arguably the most important step, because if people don't know that you are live-tweeting, no one will read your information. On the day of the public hearing (or any event), send several tweets informing followers where you'll be and what #hashtag they can follow to join the conversation. But don't just publicize your live-tweeting on Twitter. Write about it in your blog, and post it on Facebook and LinkedIn.

3. Think outside the quotes

Anyone can access meeting minutes to read what was decided. That's why the best live-tweeters take their followers inside the meeting and provide unique information that can't be found in the minutes. At the public hearing, challenge yourself to tweet about things like body language, tone of voice, and crowd reaction. Post pictures to complement your tweets. There's so much more to a public hearing than what is decided or even what the testifiers are saying. Go beyond the quotes and give your followers the priceless information they crave.

4. Be careful about quotes

It can be very difficult to quote people in 140 characters or less. Be sure to attribute all quotes and do not take them out of context.

5. Use a Twitter management application

If your tweets generate a great deal of discussion, you'll likely become overwhelmed with questions and comments from followers. When this happens, you'll need more than just the Twitter app to handle your needs. I recommend using a program like TweetDeck or HootSuite, which allow you to separate your tweets, replies, and hashtag-specific content into different categories. These applications will ease your live-tweeting experience.

6. Interact with your followers

It is a compliment when people follow your live-tweets. For that reason, be sure to acknowledge people's tweets and answer their questions whenever possible. But for every fan, there's likely to be a naysayer. As you flood the market with real-time information, some people might grow tired of reading your tweets. They might even heckle you. Ignore them (unless their criticisms are valid, of course!), and keep reminding yourself that there are people out there who appreciate what you're doing.

Writing opinion columns

Dear Ann E. Answers:

I would like to shed some light on an issue that I consider to be my area of expertise. Should I share my opinion through the newspaper? If so, should I write a letter to the editor or would it be better to write an opinion column?

Sincerely,

Expert with Opinions

Dear Expert with Opinions:

A letter to the editor is much shorter than an opinion piece. Most letters are fewer than 200 words, while an opinion piece – or "op-ed" – is usually between 500 and 700 words. Typically a letter to the editor is submitted in response to something that was previously published in the same publication, while an op-ed can introduce a thought, opinion or idea.

Whether you submit an op-ed or a letter to the editor depends on who you are. If you are an average person with an opinion, you should write a letter to the editor. If you have a unique qualification or connection to a topic, you should submit an op-ed. When you submit the piece to the editorial page or opinion editor, explain in the e-mail who you are and why you are qualified to write the column.

If you decide to submit a letter to the editor, see page 97. If you want to submit an op-ed, here are some tips on how to write an effective column.

- **Select a current and newsworthy topic.** If the topic you're writing about is not top-of-mind for news editors, it is unlikely to be published.
- **Grab readers' attention.** The first few sentences are the most important. Grab readers' attention in the first paragraph. This will also increase the chance of your piece getting published.
- **Write "tight" copy.** The 500- to 700-word count sneaks up on you faster than you'd think, and you want to make sure you say all you need to say.
- **Use conversational language.** An op-ed is not a master's thesis. It's an educated opinion piece, but should be written for the general public to read.
- **Respect readers' intelligence.** While the copy should be easy to understand, don't insult readers with over-explanations or condescending language.
- **Choose your words and tone carefully.** While you may be irate about an issue, keep your tone calm and respectful.
- **Pick a side and stick to it.** Your piece will not get published if you are wavering on an issue. Express an opinion and argue your point. If you don't have a clear viewpoint, you may want to reconsider writing the column.
- **Don't get discouraged.** If your piece is not published, don't spend too much time sulking about it. There are many factors beyond your control that editors must weigh when deciding whether to publish an op-ed. You could consider submitting it to a different newspaper or media outlet.

Submitting letters to the editor

Dear Ann E. Answers:

What is the most effective way to write and submit a letter to the editor nowadays? The last time I did, The Cosby Show *was the number one TV show in America.*

Sincerely,

Old-Timer

Dear Old-Timer:
You're right; a lot has changed since the 1980s. Back then, most letters to the editor were mailed to the newspaper. Today, "letters to the editor" are more of a figure of speech, because they are usually submitted via e-mail. This is particularly beneficial for time-sensitive topics that might not be considered newsworthy the following week.

Before you begin writing, consider the publication. Largely circulated publications receive hundreds of letters, so your odds of being published improve with a smaller publication.

Read the publication's instructions for letters to the editor. Most newspapers have their own guidelines for length, what to include, and how to submit a letter.

In general, the letter should be brief, about four to eight sentences in length. In the beginning, state whether you are responding to an article, letter, or opinion piece, and, if so, which one. Then introduce your issue. Articulate your argument with a few sentences that support your stance on the issue. Most letters to the editor close with a statement that urges readers to support or oppose an issue.

It is a good rule of thumb to not exceed 200 words. Also, even if you wish to be anonymous (which you must explicitly state), most publications will require you to provide your name, city, and a phone number. Editors will probably contact you to verify your identity before publishing the letter.

A politician's tweeting guidelines

Dear Ann E. Answers:

I have had a Twitter account for a while, but now that I am a state legislator I am unsure of what kinds of things I should tweet about. How can I engage with my constituents in a meaningful way without adding fuel to the political fire?

Sincerely,

Legislator in a Twitter

Dear Legislator in a Twitter:

Having a social media account as an elected official gives you more access to your constituents, the issues they care about, and what people are saying about you. But it can also expose you to negative criticism and hard-pressed questions. Some politicians have even committed the political equivalent of suicide because of their injudicious comments.

To avoid harming your reputation, here are two suggestions to consider before you tweet yourself into a real twitter.

- **Listen first, then talk.** Just because Twitter moves at a rapid pace doesn't mean you shouldn't think twice (or more!) before you post – especially if you are tweeting about something you passionately support or oppose. Take a deep breath, remain rational, and consider how your post may be interpreted. If you wouldn't say the comment out loud at a press conference, you shouldn't tweet it.

- **Consider the medium.** Some political discussions are not meant for Twitter. Compressing your thoughts into 140 characters is difficult. Try linking to a source such as a blog or press release to offer more information, if appropriate.

To ensure the effectiveness of your tweets, be sure to follow a political version of the Hippocratic Oath: first do no harm.

Should I respond to negative tweets?

Dear Ann E. Answers:

I am a first-time campaign manager for a state senate candidate. Part of my job is to manage social media sites. Recently my candidate has come under attack in the Twitterverse for her stance on a controversial issue. Should I respond to these negative tweets on behalf of my candidate? If so, what is the most effective way to respond?

Sincerely,

High-Road Campaigner

Dear High-Road Campaigner:

Welcome to the double-edged sword of social media. Voters have access to candidates like never before, just as candidates can now use social media as a voter contact tool. When a candidate starts a Twitter account, it opens the door for negative tweets and direct attacks, so it is important to establish and maintain a consistent response strategy. Understanding how to respond to negative tweets can help you manage your candidate's reputation and even build supporters, if handled effectively.

To answer your first question, I think you *should* respond to the tweets if they use respectful language, come from a legitimate username, and directly call out your candidate's Twitter @username. Disrespectful tweets laced with name-calling or vulgar language do not deserve the courtesy of a response. Furthermore, tweets from anonymous or fake Twitter accounts (e.g., @FakeSarahPalin) do not need to be addressed because people often start them solely for the purpose of bashing candidates or brands. Thoughtful and polite tweets from valid Twitter accounts, on the other hand, do merit a response.

Here are some tips on how to respond to such tweets.

- Establish an efficient tweet approval process with your candidate. If she wants to see all response tweets before they go live, be sure she approves before posting them.
- Respond quickly to decrease the chances of the negative tweet(s) spreading.
- Keep your cool. Using a defensive or argumentative tone will make your candidate appear unprofessional and/or unpleasant.

Here are some tips on what the tweet(s) could include.

- Thank the person for his or her input.
- Correct any inaccuracies in the tweet.
- Restate your candidate's view.
- Provide a link (if applicable) for more information.
- Try to keep your response to one tweet (less than 140 characters). If you absolutely have to send a second tweet, make sure you have it prepared in advance so you can send it immediately after the first tweet. It can get confusing for your followers when two related tweets get separated.
- If the conversation continues past three tweeted exchanges, change the venue. Send the user a private message to create a dialogue that's no longer in the public eye.

Click to Apply

Making the right impression

Interview dress code

Dear Ann E. Answers:

I'm interviewing for a new position, and I've been told that a black or navy suit is the standard for both men and women – no matter what position you are interviewing for. The person interviewing me won't be wearing a suit. Should I still wear one?

Sincerely,

Cautiously Suited

Dear Cautiously Suited:

Your wardrobe can make a strong opening statement in an interview. In general, dress for the position you want. However, if that position doesn't require a suit, it is still better to err on the safe side and wear one. Last time I checked, being over-dressed doesn't take you out of the running for most jobs. In fact, it can do quite the opposite.

Without knowing your background, how you dress can tell a lot about you. Being well-groomed and well-dressed will convey professionalism and speak to your credibility.

You don't want anything about your appearance to distract or take away from the message you are trying to send. Avoid being unshaven; wearing wrinkled clothes, a low-cut top, or a wildly patterned tie; applying too much make-up; or accessorizing with gaudy jewelry. That being said, incorporating some personality into your apparel can also help you feel more comfortable and, in turn, may help you stand out from the pack. Wear your favorite color shirt or tie, go for pinstripes, add a belt, etc. If you are called back for a second interview, it is okay to wear the same suit if you only own one – especially if you are meeting with different people. Be sure to wear a different shirt or tie, though, just in case there is some overlap.

Dressing professionally doesn't have to mean being uncomfortable. There are bases that need to be covered when it comes to looking sharp, but if you can't walk in heels, don't wear them. Part of giving a confident, professional vibe is feeling comfortable in your own skin – or clothes, in this case.

Even if you are told prior to the interview that business casual is okay, you should still dress for success. For men, wearing khakis, a dress shirt, and blazer is a safe approach to looking professional, yet casual. If you want to be taken seriously, then your appearance must literally follow suit.

Other nonverbal communication skills, like eye contact, are also important during an interview (see page 18).

According to a 2006 National Association of Colleges and Employees (NACE) survey, 87% of employers who recruit new college graduates said that a candidate's overall appearance influences their opinion about the candidate. This is the most recent data available.

National Association of Colleges and Employees, "Job Outlook 2006," (2006).

Resume facelift

Dear Ann E. Answers:

I'm mid-career, a little worried about my current job, and starting to think I should look elsewhere. My resume desperately needs a facelift. While I know what skills and positions to highlight in my resume, I'm not sure how I should lay out the text. Some people have recommended that I use a non-traditional resume format, while others advise that I follow traditional guidelines. What do you think is the best way to present myself on paper?

Sincerely,

Puzzled Resume Writer

Dear Puzzled Resume Writer:

There are two elements to a resume: layout and content. At a glance, potential employers notice a resume's layout first, but overall they care much more about the content. Unless you are in a creativity-based industry, such as design, music, advertising, or film, where originality is encouraged, stick to the basics. White paper, black ink, one-inch margins, and a professional font sized between 10 point and 12 point are general guidelines to follow.

That being said, multimedia resumes are becoming more prominent. If you provide an electronic version of your resume, you could include your LinkedIn and Twitter handles and embed writing samples or videos into your resume.

Typically, resumes include name and contact information at the top; a summary of the candidate's background and experience in one or two sentences;

a work experience section highlighting current and previous job experience and tasks; and education and ongoing training/leadership information.

Be mindful of your word selection. Many employers sift through resumes using keywords. Certain words can be advantageous, while others might damage your chances. For example, words that exemplify ownership over a project or leadership over people, like *manage, author, direct, oversee, lead, facilitate, generate* or *develop*, grab the attention of potential employers. However, using them is not enough; you also need to demonstrate the result or outcome. Also, keep your tone active instead of passive. For example, replace "Researching complex statistics was an integral part of my job" with "I frequently researched complex statistics and compiled thoughtful reports."

The content is the most important part of your resume. Tweaking your resume to align with the position's description of what they are looking for in a candidate will help send your resume to the top of the stack.

According to LinkedIn, the top 10 terms that job seekers overuse in their resumes are creative, organizational, effective, motivated, extensive experience, track record, innovative, responsible, analytical, and problem solving.

LinkedIn Blog, "Top 10 Overused Professional Buzzwords 2012," (December 4, 2012).

Recommending a colleague

Dear Ann E. Answers:

A young woman whom I supervise at work has asked me to write a recommendation letter for her. I'm happy to recommend her, but I'm short on time and don't know where to begin. Help!

Sincerely,

Lost for Words

Dear Lost for Words:

Don't stress out! Here's how to write a thoughtful recommendation letter in 8-10 sentences.

1. Establish how you know the person. *Jane assisted me on the communications team at Company A for two years.*

2. If appropriate, set a positive tone for why the person is moving on. *We were sad when Jane left to pursue a master's degree, but are excited that she is pursuing her dream of working in the museum community, where I know her passion lies.*

3. Highlight the person's impressive qualities and skills, and provide specific examples if possible. *Jane is a gifted communicator. At Company A, she delivered consistently strong marketing and media materials, including a philanthropy blog and brochure for one client whose president called them "better than he could have ever imagined." Jane took on projects with enthusiasm and handled them with detail from start to finish. She was a self-starter and could easily handle many tasks at the same time.*

4. Indicate what potential employers would like and appreciate about this person. *Jane is the kind of strategic thinker that organizations need to achieve a higher level of success. She will do well in whatever she wants to do, and she will earn the respect of her peers.*

5. Invite follow-up questions. *If you would like to discuss Jane's capabilities further, please call me at 123-456-7890.*

Censoring your Facebook and Twitter pages

Dear Ann E. Answers:

I'm graduating from college in a few months, which means my life will soon be taken over by job applications. I have been told that many employers look at the Facebook accounts of applicants. Is this true? If so, what types of things should I remove from my Facebook account before applying for jobs?

Sincerely,

Carefree Facebooker

Dear Carefree Facebooker:

Your sources are correct. Many employers look at Facebook pages as part of their screening process. But since you don't know which ones do and which ones don't, you should assume that every employer will look at your Facebook page. Why wouldn't they? If you were the manager of a company, wouldn't you want to know the character and habits of the people you are considering for the job?

Since you have spent your last four (or more) years in college, you probably have plenty of Facebook housekeeping to do. Below are items you should include on your list of chores.

- **Remove inappropriate pictures**. If there are any pictures of you on Facebook doing something unprofessional or irresponsible, untag or delete them. If someone else posted the pictures, kindly ask them to remove them. In my opinion, a picture of you having a drink with friends in a responsible setting is perfectly acceptable. Conversely, a picture of you dancing on the table at a keg party should be deleted. If you're unsure, err on the side of removing it.

- **Manage your language.** Take a look at your Facebook timeline and remove any posts with obscene, discriminatory or grammatically incorrect language.
- **Practice good writing.** If you demonstrate poor writing skills on your Facebook page, companies might make assumptions about your grasp of the English language.
- **Be polite.** Don't bad-mouth other people on Facebook. Employers don't like backstabbers and gossipers.
- **Strengthen your privacy settings.** Make sure your privacy settings allow only your friends to view status updates and photos you post to your timeline. A Facebook page that is open to the public shows carelessness and a lack of social media discretion.
- **When you apply for a job, search for the company on Facebook.** If they have a page, "like" it and browse the timeline for more information. And don't worry, when you "like" a company's Facebook page, it does not automatically give the company added access to your personal page.

Finally, the online housekeeping doesn't end with your Facebook page. Do you have a personal blog or Twitter account? You should give your entire online image a once-over to eliminate the risk of it costing you the chance at a good job. You're not in college anymore. You're a professional. Your Facebook page should reflect that. Now go out there and get that job!

According to a Microsoft study, 70% of employers in the United States have turned down a potential job candidate based solely on the candidate's online reputation.

Microsoft, "Online Reputation," (December 2009).

Maintaining professionalism on Facebook

Dear Ann E. Answers:

I was reprimanded at work recently for posting something negative about my job on Facebook. My supervisor said that if I do it again, I will be fired. This is incredibly unfair. What I do or say in my personal life shouldn't have any consequences at work, right?

Sincerely,

Unfairly Punished

Dear Unfairly Punished:

Sounds like you need a wake-up call. Your private time is your private time, as long as you aren't publicly posting negative comments about your employer on the Internet. You are a representative of your company, so your employer has an interest in ensuring that you don't tarnish its image. Many companies have policies regarding social media – check with your human resources department. If you have a problem with your company, be proactive – you're more likely to solve your problems if you talk with your supervisor rather than your social media buddies.

While you – and most of us – certainly like the freedom to express our thoughts and ideas, you need to understand the impact of your actions. Many companies monitor their employees' social media activity. If you don't like it, strengthen the privacy settings on your page – or keep your commentary offline.

Grumbling about your job or your boss *in private* is an age-old human privilege. But social media by definition is a form of *public* communication.

Of companies with 1,000 or more employees:

- 20% reported having issues with employees' use of social media
- 7% reported dismissing someone for their behavior on social media sites

Proofpoint, "Outbound E-mail and DLP Survey," (2010).

In response to the Occupy movement protest nearby, a corporation sent memos cautioning employees not to engage protesters. However, a temporary worker disregarded these memos and commented on the protesters' Facebook page about the power-washing of the company's windows. She called the window cleaning a waste of time and money. Due to this post, the temporary worker was promptly fired for disregarding company policy.

Jennifer Bjorhus, "U.S. Bank Temp Says Occupy Post Got Her Fired," Star Tribune, (November 4, 2011).

Further help

From social media posts to conference calls to handwritten thank-you notes, I have tried to provide the tried-and-true rules which govern business communications today. If you are confounded by another communications etiquette problem, please e-mail me at anneanswers@goffpublic.com.

For guidance on business etiquette and social manners more generally, you may find the following books helpful.

- Alford, Henry, *Would It Kill You to Stop Doing That: A Modern Guide to Manners* (New York: Twelve, 2012).
- Galanes, Philip, *Social Q's: How to Survive the Quirks, Quandaries and Quagmires of Today* (New York: Simon & Schuster, 2011).
- Post, Peggy, Anna Post, Lizzie Post, and Daniel Post Senning, *Emily Post's Etiquette, 18th Edition: Manners for a New World* (New York: HarperCollins, 2011).
- Smith, Jodi, *The Etiquette Book: A Complete Guide to Modern Manners* (New York: Sterling, 2011).
- Whitmore, Jacqueline, *Business Class: Etiquette Essentials for Success at Work* (New York: St. Martin's Press, 2005).

Acknowledgments

Like most successful public relations efforts, Ann E. Answers and her book of advice columns are the result of collaboration – in this case, one involving all of the employees of Goff Public.

The genesis was a brainstorming session by our social media team about etiquette mistakes in business, social media, and politics. This soon led to a post on *The GP Spin* (goffpublic.com/blog), our company blog, under the byline of Miss E-Manners, a perfect parodic name for our advice dispenser.

One blog post quickly turned into more, as the entire Goff Public team identified other common etiquette mistakes. Our company president soon suggested that the blog posts might as well be rounded out and published in book form, given the wealth of communications *faux pas* to set right.

Miss E-Manners, however, was open to an all-too-characteristic possible threat in the present age: the potential of a lawsuit. After consulting with a top intellectual property lawyer, we renamed our advice dispenser Ann E. Answers.

We are fortunate to have in-house experts in writing, production, and public relations who all worked together to make this book possible.

In addition to the work of Goff Public employees, this

book benefitted from outside advice. A special thanks is owed to Jodi R.R. Smith, president of Mannersmith Etiquette Consulting, for providing feedback on our manuscript.

Proceeds from this book will be donated to Dress for Success, a nonprofit organization which provides business attire, interview skills, and job retention support to help economically disadvantaged women achieve self-sufficiency. For more information for Dress for Success, visit dressforsuccess.org/twincities.

About Ann E. Answers

Ann E. Answers is the embodiment of a young professional who is fed up with the mistakes that she sees in business communications. She takes a sensible, practical approach to communications etiquette. As a city girl who grew up in a rural community, Ann E. Answers dispenses etiquette advice with a combination of down-to-earth sensibilities and urban sophistication. When she's not dispensing etiquette advice, she's serving on local boards and giving to nonprofits.

About Goff Public

Goff Public is a public relations and public affairs firm based in Saint Paul, Minnesota, with a Midwestern and national clientele. Its professionals help clients communicate with policymakers, community groups, internal audiences, and the general public. Its services include strategic message development, social media, traditional media relations, crisis communications, lobbying, coalition building, and community relations. To learn more, please visit www.goffpublic.com.

Index

CPSIA information can be obtained at www.ICGtesting.com
Printed in the USA
BVOW07s0302061213

338320BV00008B/103/P

9 781626 522985